The Day The Capitol Burned

February 5, 1911

With A Brief Pictorial Review
of the Development
of Missouri and its Capitols

By Joseph S. Summers, Jr.

CeMoMedServ Publications
516 E. Capitol Avenue, #E
Jefferson City, Missouri 65101
Copyright 1986 CeMoMedServ Publications
All rights reserved
Printed in the United States of America

Library of Congress Cataloging Card Number: 86-70675

ISBN 0-916109-04-6

Contents

Preface

Through history, fire has claimed many valuable treasures. Missouri government has fallen victim to the ravages of fire on more than one occasion. The first Missouri State Capitol Building in Jefferson City was destroyed by fire in 1837. And February 5, 1986, marked the 75th Anniversary of the fire that destroyed the second Missouri State Capitol Building in Jefferson City.

The 1911 Capitol fire was a significant event in the history of our state. True, efforts were underway to replace the 71-year-old structure. But a lightning bolt began a flame which, in two days, accomplished what it may have taken another ten years to agree upon.

In a state of shock, Missouri salvaged what it could, and worked together to build a new Capitol. This book attempts to recapture the drama of the events that followed one lightning bolt.

Acknowledgments

This book is the product of a team effort. My staff has participated to the extent that the "author" is no longer the writer, but instead has become the team leader. LuAnn Frevert assisted in researching, writing, editing and typing. Terri Boyce, in addition to typing, handled the gathering of photographs and illustrations, and the final layout of the text. John Robinson served as an editor, writer, and production consultant.

Joseph R. Kroeger, Sr., has provided many photographs. His assistance in securing additional reference sources, his attention to detail and his enthusiasm were invaluable.

Rep. Gladys Marriott (D-Independence) supplied the cover photo, courtesy of the Independence Fire Department.

We are indebted to the *Jefferson City News Tribune* for an article published in the *Post Tribune* on February 5, 1952. "Today is Anniversary of Burning of Second State Capitol Building" was a major reference source for Part I - The Fire. The *Sedalia Democrat-Sentinel* of February 6, 1911, was also invaluable in our research, as were news items from Kirksville, St. Louis and Kansas City newspapers.

Sources for Parts II and III include the *Jeffersonian Republican* and the *Peoples Tribune,* Jefferson City newspapers of the 1800s; *An Illustrated History of Missouri* by Walter B. Davis and Daniel S. Durrie (1876); and *The State of Missouri* by Walter Williams (1904). An article entitled "Capitol Burns in 1911" published in the 1968 Capital City Telephone Directory (author unknown) also played an integral part in the development of these sections, especially "The Third Capitol -1917."

John Viessman, staff artist for the Missouri State Museum of the Department of Natural Resources, shared eyewitness accounts of the fire and copies of several newspaper articles; as did Mrs. Mary Gamble, who contributed copies of 1911 Jefferson City newspapers. The Missouri State Archives provided copies of documents relating to Parts II and III.

The photographs and illustrations were provided by Joseph R. Kroeger, Sr., Ron Arsenault, the Cole County Historical Society, the Missouri State Museum of the Department of Natural Resources, the Missouri State Archives, the State Historical Society, the Sanborn Maps of 1908 and 1916, and *Suden's Souvenir of Jefferson City, MO.*

Several other individuals have also contributed pictures, ideas and odd facts. To all the named and unnamed sources, I give my deepest, most heartfelt thanks.

For a more comprehensive study of this area in Missouri's history, I highly recommend *The History of Missouri Capitols* by Marian M. Ohman.

Part I

The Capitol Burns

(Illustrated Sketch Book and Directory of Jefferson City and Cole County Missouri 19

The remodeled 1840 Capitol as it appeared before the devastating fire. The gates opened onto Stewart Street.

The Fire

It was Sunday evening February 5, 1911. The latter part of January and the early part of February had been unusually warm. A thunderstorm was brewing. A menacing black cloud blocked the western sky, announcing its steady advance on Jefferson City with brilliant, crackling flashes of lightning.

In *Women of the Mansion, 1821-1936,* First Lady Mrs. Herbert S. Hadley remembers that fateful evening:

> Around six o'clock Sunday evening, February 5, 1911, I sat writing at the desk in the bay-window of my bedroom, when there was a sudden stroke of lightning which, for a moment, I thought must have hit the Mansion. I continued my writing, and some time later flame began to trickle out of the dome of the Capitol. The lightning had struck there instead of the Mansion. I cannot describe the night of confusion that followed . . . Lights in the Mansion went out, and how large and dark the place seemed until the flames glared in! There was no sleep for anyone that night.

Mrs. Kathryn Sinclair Hammond lived less than one block from the Capitol at 221 Stewart Street. She recalls, "It was just about dark. I could see a glow at the top of the dome that looked like a candle burning."

According to Mrs. Hadley, the bolt of lightning struck around 6:00 p.m. Local press and historians have recorded the time at approximately 7:00 p.m., and the *Sedalia Democrat-Sentinel* recorded the time as 8:00

p.m. The latter, however, seems a definite error, since all other accounts recorded the 6:00 and 7:00 o'clock times.

The structure of the dome seemed custom-made for a lightning bolt's handiwork. The 130-foot dome of the 1840 Capitol was completely remodeled in 1887-1888, increasing the height to 185 feet. A base of stonework supported the upper hemispherical portion, which was constructed of pine timbers. Metal sheathing enclosed the pine frame. A lantern (the small decorative windowed structure), complete with an outside observation walkway, crowned the dome.

Another eyewitness, Monsignor Joseph Selinger is quoted in the *Missouri Valley Fire Chief's Journal* for April and May of 1951, page 28:

> I was standing on the front steps of the hospital [St. Mary's] about 5:30 when a heavy cloud from the west seemed to hiss with lightning, followed by peals of thunder. One flash struck the four armed electric wires [lightning rod] on the lantern of the dome, which had long since been dismantled. I walked home toward St. Peter's Church after the rain let up. The inside of the dome gradually filled with smoke. The lightning had ignited the dead wires. The wood soon began to burn, and fell to the base.

Several accounts of the fire's discovery were reported. According to a *Jefferson City Post Tribune* article of February 5, 1952, the eerie yellow glow from inside the top of the Capitol dome was first seen by persons walking along Main Street (now Capitol Avenue). One witness on Main Street rushed to call a telephone operator, who notified the fire department.

The *Kirksville Democrat* of February 10, 1911, and the *Sedalia Daily*

Capitol reported that the fire was discovered by boys who were playing on the Capitol grounds. These accounts indicate that the boys ran to the Madison House hotel and gave the alarm.

The *Jefferson City Capital News,* February 6, 1911, tells:

> Mrs. George Monhardt, who resides on Broadway, discovered the fire and turned in the alarm.

The fire bell rang and the local volunteer fire departments, under Chief Ed Gray, responded at once with fire hose carts, located in four areas of the city. The Central Station was in the basement of City Hall on the corner of Monroe and High Streets, the Richmond Hill Volunteer Fire Department was at 116 Bolivar Street, the Muenichberg Fire Department was on the corner of Washington and Dunklin Streets, and a fourth hose shed was located at Clark Avenue and Miller Street.

Libby Tihen, whose father was proprietor of the John Tihen Livery Stable at 315 Jefferson Street, remembers that King and Deck were the horses trained to run under a "swinging harness" at the sound of the fire bell. She recalls, "When they heard those fire bells ring, there wasn't any holding them. When the bells rang, they were going."

Governor Herbert S. Hadley was entertaining approximately 30 newsmen at the Mansion when Pardon Attorney W. L. Chambers, who was in the governor's office at the Capitol, notified him that the Capitol building was on fire. The governor and newsmen left at once for the Capitol.

When the governor reached the Capitol and surveyed the situation, he ran to his office to telephone Henry Andrae, the state prison warden, to bring the prison fire hoses, all the guards he could spare, and all the trustee prisoners who were trained in fire fighting. Shortly after 8:00 p.m., Deputy Warden Gilvin and twelve black convicts arrived to help the city fire department.

The governor then called National Guard Adjutant General Frank M. Rumbold. Research compiled by Orval L. Henderson, Jr., entitled "Militia at the Fire," states that the governor gave a verbal order to call out Company L, Second Infantry Regiment "for general guard duty and to assist in the salvage of property and records." Company L was a "bare bones" cadre of volunteers with a roster of 27 enlisted men. Seventeen arrived for duty (four were out of town attending college, and six others did not report). Major Paul C. Hunt, an officer in the quartermaster corps, served as the temporary commanding officer (rather than a lieutenant of the infantry who would normally command such a group). The men were dressed in khaki uniforms with rubber service coats.

Those reporting for duty were:

William S. Moore	Thomas H. Cromley
Robert E. Holliway	Cecil H. Engelbrecht
Clifford Porth	John H. Eppenaner
Ludwick Graves	Hugo Monnig, Jr.
Justin Enloe	Lucian E. Pippinger
Arthur Scott	Linn R. Stanforth
Frederick W. Robinson	Earl E. Silvey
Phillip A. Conrath	Frederick H. Zeith
Paul C. Hunt	

Governor Hadley called the superintendent of the Missouri Pacific Railroad for a squad of their employees to leave the tracks below, climb the hill, and help with the rescue attempts. The Lincoln Institute volunteer fire department also joined the efforts.

The firemen, unable to fight the fire from inside the dome, crashed through the doors and ran out onto the roof over the Senate and House chambers. The fire gained ground very slowly during the first hour, continuing to spread through the dried supporting pine rafters of the 71-year-old structure.

During the term of Mayor Phillip Ott (1889-1891), the city had voted for a water works, and fire hydrants were installed. The water system installed was a direct pressure system with a small water tower as a reserve. The water pressure was insufficient from this system to spray water 185 feet to the top of the Capitol dome. Even if the pressure had been sufficient, it would have been impossible to penetrate the waterproof metal sheathing surrounding the dome. In effect, the dome had become a woodstove, with a blazing wood frame within a metal casing.

The inadequate water pressure is emphasized in a story in the *St. Louis Post Dispatch,* February 6, 1911:

> A line of hose was carried into the tower on a long winding stairway, but when the water was turned on, it would not run from the nozzle. In the meantime, the fire protection hose in the Capitol was carried into the dome. Water would not run from this. It was then found that a valve in the basement was cut off. When this was turned on, a small stream ran from the hose but it was not enough to affect the blaze which, by this time, had enveloped the entire cupola.

The upper portion of the Capitol dome collapsed and set fire to the roof over the House of Representatives. The flames soon roared through the rotunda and the entire second floor.

To add to the problem of water pressure, the ladders reaching to the top of the dome were too weak to support a fireman and a heavy hose.

The firefighters thought that when the fire descended to the level where the water hoses could be used effectively, the fire could be checked.

The metal sheathing on the dome gave warning that it was about to collapse as it showered flaming fragments on the roof below. The firemen moved back on the roof.

At 8:30 p.m. the wooden timbers supporting the metal sheathing crumbled and the upper portion of the dome toppled onto the north side of the Capitol, setting fire to the roof over the House of Representatives. Timbers also fell to the floor of the rotunda, covering the inlaid state seal. The firemen remained on the roof using all 15 available hoses until the flames became so hot that the men were forced to abandon the area.

At the time the flaming metal sheaths of the dome crashed and fell through the roof of the older central section, the firefighters encountered a unique problem. When the Capitol was remodeled in 1887-1888, the wings on the north and south ends of the building were higher than the 1840 central portion of the building. A false upper roof was added to make the entire roof the same level. Neither roof was fireproof since they were supported by pine timbers. When the fire spread to this area between the old and new roofs, the firemen were further hampered because there was no access to the area. Burning timbers from the roofs then collapsed, setting fire to the wooden floors of the older central portion of the building. The rotunda and the dome area became one large chimney.

Flames shot one hundred feet above the building and were visible for 20 miles up and down the river.

According to the *St. Louis Post Dispatch,* at this time the fire could be seen for 20 miles up and down the river, far into Callaway and Boone Counties:

> The flames lighted brilliantly the sky darkened by black clouds, but at times illuminated by flashes of lightning from the storm.

Mrs. Alma Ruth Pearre Meyer recalls, "I was almost six years old at the time of the fire. We lived ten miles east of here in Callaway County, close to where the race track [Capital Speedway, Holts Summit] is now. We watched from a second-story porch, and could see the flames."

Local accounts indicate that the long-distance phone lines were busy as operators answered questions from those within sight of the flames.

After the dome crumbled, the work force began moving records in earnest. Jefferson City Chief of Police Anton Richter kept idle spectators out of the way and prevented the doors and steps from becoming blocked. Reports estimate that the state records were saved by approximately 600 persons, including two-thirds of the male population of Jefferson City, and all available members of the legislature (34 Senators and 142 Representatives), which was in session.

Robert McClintic, Secretary of the Senate, was able to move all but a few of the more current, less valuable papers. According to the February 6, 1911, issue of the *Kansas City Post,* McClintic narrowly escaped the collapse of a skylight, grabbing a tin bucket to use as a helmet to protect him from the flying glass. Others followed his example using willow

(Cole County Historical Society)

A human chain was formed to rescue and transport the state records from Secretary of State Cornelius Roach's office to the Supreme Court building (foreground).

baskets for protection. A few received minor cuts from the glass.

Senator Mike Casey of Kansas City was gathering his personal effects in the Senate chamber when he noticed the George Caleb Bingham paintings of George Washington and Thomas Jefferson. He suggested to his collegues that they save the paintings. Afterwards, the *Kansas City Post* quoted him as saying:

> I couldn't have felt like a good Democrat if I had failed to rescue Tom Jefferson.

Because the dome fell to the north over the House of Representatives chamber, very little was saved from that area.

The *Sedalia Democrat-Sentinel* describes the remarkable feat accomplished by Secretary of State Cornelius Roach. He organized a human chain from his office to the old Supreme Court building on the Capitol grounds, and at 8:30 p.m., they began moving records, including valuable land records and the great seal of the state. In 40 minutes, all the records were removed except those in a fireproof time vault. The vault contained, among other things, $20,000 cash, $500,000 in school bonds, and $100,000 in legislative script.

The governor was assisted in removing his office papers by Pardon Attorney W. L. Chambers, his private secretary, Charles Thompson, and two stenographers, Mrs. Mary Leo and Sam Haley.

The *Sedalia Democrat-Sentinel* describes the scene of organized confusion:

> Desks were tumbled down the long stairway leading to the building, books were thrown about topsy turvy, and in thirty minutes the south side of the Capitol park was an indiscriminate mass of books, papers and furniture. Wagons drove back and forth gathering up load after load, and long rows of men carried the removable property into the old Supreme Court building.

At 8:43 p.m., John F. "King" Heinrichs, a prominent furniture dealer and mayor of Jefferson City, called the mayor of Sedalia, J. W. Mellor, asking for the help of their steam engine pump.

At 9:10 p.m., the House chamber roof crashed. Soon the entire older section of the building and the second floor of the new section were in flames. The fire was contained on the second floor of the new wings, since the floors were fireproof.

Meanwhile, a special Missouri Pacific train prepared to leave Sedalia for the capital. It included an engine, a caboose, two flat cars for the equipment and a coach for the firemen, newsmen and a few outsiders. On this special train were Fire Chief W. H. Paul, four assistants, conductor Walter Mann, trainmaster C. M. Hunt, engineer John Overmier, the steam engine pump and a hose cart from Company 2. With a clear track, the train left Sedalia at 10:18 p.m. One hour and 14 minutes later it reached Cole Junction on the outskirts of Jefferson City, four miles from the Capitol. According to the *Sedalia Democrat-Sentinel,* the total run to Jefferson City of approximately 63 miles was accomplished in 78 minutes, a record for the period.

(*Missouri State Museum*)

Sedalia's Fire Company No. 2 arrived in Jefferson City on a special Missouri Pacific train.

When the Sedalia firemen arrived Sunday at midnight, they thought the fire was dying. However, because of a break in the water main, it continued to burn for another 36 hours.

Although it was first believed by the Sedalia firemen that the fire had almost burned itself out by the time they arrived Sunday near midnight, this was not true. The fire continued to burn until Tuesday morning. The Sedalia fire department was indeed great help. The steam pumper produced a water pressure so strong that Chief Paul was quoted in the Sedalia newspaper:

> Two men were required to hold the hoses and direct them. [At that time] seven streams of water were playing on the ruins in an effort to keep the safe and vault areas as cool as possible.

Fireman Joseph Frank was carried from the building suffering from smoke inhalation, but revived upon reaching fresh air. A penitentiary inmate known as "Bear Clay" was also overcome by heat and smoke and carried out.

National Guard Major Paul Hunt was one of the last to leave the building.

At 4:00 a.m. a break occurred in the water main, which forced the firemen to stand by helplessly for almost 24 hours with only a trickle of water.

National Guard records indicate that a part of a stone wall fell on a fire hose. The resultant back pressure may have caused the break.

However, John Sturm, a young Jefferson City resident at the time, remembers that "the water company put the pressure on the pumps at the pumphouse down on the river where they pumped the water from the river. By putting the pressure on, they broke the water main up in the 800 block of West Main Street, and they lost their pressure."

(Missouri State Archives)

(State Historical Society of Missour

Monday morning's light revealed the gutted interior of the Capitol.

After the water main burst, the fire burned from one room to the next. Rapid burning of the pine shelves in the basement had been anticipated, but tons of leatherbound volumes slowed the flames. In some cases, a shelf of books toppling on a big blaze temporarily smothered it.

Insofar as possible, salvage of records continued through Monday, February 6. The *Springfield Leader* of that date reports:

> About 40 convicts from the Missouri penitentiary were at work in the ruins of the burned building today, carrying the remains of the records to places of safety. None of them has attempted to make an escape and all entered upon the work zealously.

After extinguishing a burning basement door, the workers discovered that 400 gallons of explosive disinfectant had been stored behind it. John Scott, the commissioner of the permanent seat of government, said, "If the fire had gotten to the disinfectant, the blast would surely have killed all of the workmen working in and around the ruins and some of the spectators." At the time at least 30 men were carrying books from the basement.

(Cole County Historical Society)

About noon it was possible to check the time vault that
contained the money and valuable papers. The contents
were found intact.

With no water in the water main, Sedalia's steam pump was of no use. Monday morning the Sedalia firemen were taken to the Madison House hotel for breakfast, compliments of Mayor Heinrichs. He personally thanked them for their speedy response to the emergency. They then boarded the special train at 8:00 a.m. and returned to Sedalia. An article in the *Sedalia Democrat-Sentinel* of February 7, 1911, states that the train cost the State of Missouri $126 or roughly $1 per mile.

On Tuesday morning, February 7, 1911, after the water supply was restored, the fire was quickly put out, but the damage was done, and the building was a total loss.

An editorial in the *Jefferson City Democrat-Tribune* written by editor Joseph Goldman mourned the loss of the impressive Capitol, but he said such an end for it was not unexpected. Architects who had inspected it and local residents who, as young people, had played in the dusty rafters under the roof, knew that if fire ever broke out in the upper part of the building, nothing could be done to prevent its spread.

The Aftermath

The ruins of the Capitol lay bare, open to the cold front that moved in early Monday morning. Papers were scattered about the lawn of the Capitol, and a drizzling rain added to the desolate appearance.

(Cooper Photo Owned by Dr. J. S. Summers, Jr.)

Above: Egerton Swartwout, architect of the present Capitol, remarked "The ruins, what was left from the fire, were as picturesque as those of any old castle I've ever seen." (*The Architectural Record*, February 1927)

Opposite: February 14, 1911, *Jefferson City Daily Post:* "The dome of the Capitol crashed in last night during the rain at 9 o'clock. It seems that the rain loosened the mortar and the historic old dome caved in. The three crashes were heard all over the city. Architects examined the dome only a few days ago and were of the opinion that it was firm and that there was no danger of it falling in."

(Cole County Historical Socie

St. Peter's Hall was used by the House of Representatives for the remainder of the 1911 session.

When the legislature convened later that morning, the fire was still burning. The Senate met in the Cole County Courthouse on East High Street. The House of Representatives met in the Jefferson Theatre. Also known as the Jefferson Opera House, it was located behind the first three buildings from the northeast corner of High and Jefferson Street.

After Monday, the Senate found temporary quarters in the newly-constructed (1905) Supreme Court Building on West High Street, and the House of Representatives met in St. Peters Hall on West High Street. The *Jefferson City Post* of February 7, 1911, described the renovation of the hall into a legislative chamber:

> The stage will be removed and a speaker's rostrum erected in place thereof. The members will leave for St. Louis tonight to get furniture for the new legislative chamber and Rep. Irwin said this afternoon that by Monday the members will be installed and ready for business at St. Peter's Hall. The school rooms below will be converted into committee rooms and school will probably be dismissed during the balance of the session. Father Selinger went to St. Louis last night to get Archbishop Glennon's consent to dismiss school.

Classrooms for St. Peter's school were set up in nearby buildings.

The legislature used St. Peter's Hall and the Supreme Court Building during the remainder of the three-month session of the 46th General Assembly. At that time, the legislature convened in January of odd numbered years, so by the time the 47th General Assembly convened in January 1913, construction of the temporary Capitol was finished.

Some of the items recovered from the fire include slate roof tiles, floor tiles, stone rubble, and doorknobs, lockplates and a hinge from Governor Hadley's office. The Bingham portrait of Thomas Jefferson was given to the State Historical Society in Columbia. The location of Bingham's portrait of George Washington is unknown.

The heroism of the convicts from the state penitentiary was commended by the legislature and pardon recommended for those who participated. All the records may not be available, but at least four convicts who participated were paroled. As listed in the appendix to the *House and Senate Journals of the 47th General Assembly of the State of Missouri, 1913,* the names and dates of parolees included: Ned Henry, February 16, 1911; John Trigg, February 17, 1911; William Wedley, February 23, 1911; and Harrison ("Bear") Clay, February 26, 1911.

Jonas Viles, a state historian, reached Jefferson City from Columbia about noon on Monday, February 6. He obtained permission to remove the water-soaked frozen papers to the State Historical Society in Columbia to be dried, cleaned and sorted. They proved to be valuable, and included many of the records of the state conventions and legislative documents of the 1840s and 1860s.

In a paper delivered to the American Historical Association (Annual Report Number 1, 1911, pages 337-342) Jonas Viles gave a report on the "Lessons to be Drawn from the Fire in the State Capitol, Jefferson City." He not only described the fire, but he also drew conclusions for future governmental action.

Mr. Viles recalled that the first erected state Capitol in Jefferson City, built in 1826, was destroyed by fire in 1837 with a loss of valuable records in the secretary of state's office. He stated that this fire should have been a lesson to the legislature and the people of the state.

Although the legislature did request that the 1840 Capitol be constructed in a fireproof manner, the dome, the roof and the floors of this structure were not fireproof. The 1887-1888 wings added to the 1840 structure had fireproof floors, but the roof beams were constructed of wood. In addition, the continuous hallways (with no fire doors), the open halls for the legislature on the second floor, and the open rotunda made the Capitol such a poor risk that no insurance company would consider insuring either the Capitol or its contents.

The present Capitol is constructed of brick, stone and concrete, and has an all-steel frame. Although the building itself meets fireproof requirements, protection of the contents is a source of concern.

Mr. Viles summarized the lessons to be learned:

1)   The first lesson perhaps is that nothing but a grinding necessity will wring a new Capitol building from a reluctant people. The unsatisfactory and dangerous character of the old Capitol was well known to the leaders in the State; several attempts had been made to secure a new one, culminating last year [1910] in a State-wide campaign for a constitutional amendment authorizing the necessary loan. It failed, although it had no open organized opposition.

2)   Much of a practical nature can be done without great expense or radical change, to render more secure the state archives in Capitol buildings of poor fire-resisting construction in towns with inadequate fire departments.

3) [It is necessary] that the official in general charge of the Capitol
    building be a permanent appointee chosen with some regard for
    his qualifications for the post. It should be the duty of such a
    permanent appointee to be responsible for an accurate knowledge
    of the construction of the building and with the location and
    general character of the records. He would then be in a position to
    judge quickly and accurately the chances of checking any fire that
    might start, and to take charge of the removal of the records with
    intelligence and authority.

4) The state should cooperate with the town in the matter of fire
    protection. This may take the form of a contribution toward the
    cost of maintaining a permanent, well-trained department and the
    purchase of apparatus, or the installation of a supplementary
    high-pressure system for state buildings.

5) At present, perhaps, we can do no better service for the future than
    in considering and solving these very elementary problems.

Necessity did provide a new state house for the people of Missouri.
On August 1, 1911, a state-wide election was held to approve the
continuation of the seat of government in Jefferson City and to
authorize issuance of bonds for $3.5 million to erect a new Capitol. The
propositions carried, and Jefferson City held a Capitol Day celebration
on August 7, 1911.

(Bill and Mary Gamble)

The whole city turned out to watch the raging blaze. One spectator recounted, "The fire laddies took their lives in their hands as they stood beneath the blazing dome." A year after the fire (1912) the fire department modernized with the purchase of a motorized vehicle.

Part II

Missouri and Statehood

Forging Missouri's Borders

Louisiana Purchase

On October 26, 1803, an act of Congress authorized President Thomas Jefferson to take possession of the Louisiana Purchase. The formal transfer took place December 20, 1803. France had ceded this land, totaling 827,987 square miles,[1] to the United States for $15 million in the Louisiana Purchase Treaty signed April 30, 1803.

Territorial Government

On March 26, 1804, Congress divided Louisiana into two separate territories, using the 33rd parallel as the boundary (the southern boundary of the present State of Arkansas).[2] South of the 33rd parallel was the Territory of Orleans (which became the State of Louisiana in April 1812),[3] and north of the 33rd parallel was the District of Louisiana in the Territory of Indiana. Upper Louisiana, as it was named, included a vast range of country now known as Arkansas, Missouri, Iowa and the western part of Minnesota. The people of the District of Louisiana did not want to be governed by the Territory of Indiana, and presented a formal protest. Amos Stoddard, the first American governor of Upper Louisiana,[4] occupied the Government House on present day Main Street, near Walnut in St. Louis. It was used during Stoddard's seven months as governor.[5]

35

*(Sketch from **The History of Missouri** by David A. March)*

The Government House in St. Louis was used in 1804 by Upper Louisiana's first territorial governor, Amos Stoddard.

The next year, on March 3, 1805, the *District* of Louisiana became the *Territory* of Louisiana. This territory separated from the Territory of Indiana, and was named a first class territory with St. Louis as the capital.[6] The new territory had to progress through a system of first, second and third class status in order to achieve statehood.[7] As a first class territory, the people still had no voice in government.

On June 4, 1812, the Territory of Louisiana was reorganized under the name Territory of Missouri. This elevated the Missouri Territory to second class status. The people now had a say in their own government; they could vote and create a bill of rights. On the second Monday in November 1812, a delegate to Congress and representatives of the lower house were elected. The House of Representatives was apportioned at the ratio of one member for every five hundred free white male inhabitants. The nine members of the upper house, the Legislative Council, were appointed by the president to serve five-year terms.

In 1816, the Territory of Missouri became a third class territory. Citizens now elected both houses of the legislature. One member from each of the nine counties was elected to the Legislative Council.

On March 1, 1819, the Territory of Arkansas was formed from the southern portion of the Territory of Missouri. (The State of Arkansas was admitted to the Union on June 15, 1836.)[8] Iowa and the western portion of Minnesota remained part of the Territory of Missouri until 1821 when they became part of the unorganized territory of the United States.[9]

The Territory of Missouri maintained the third class status until August 1821 when the State of Missouri was admitted to the Union.

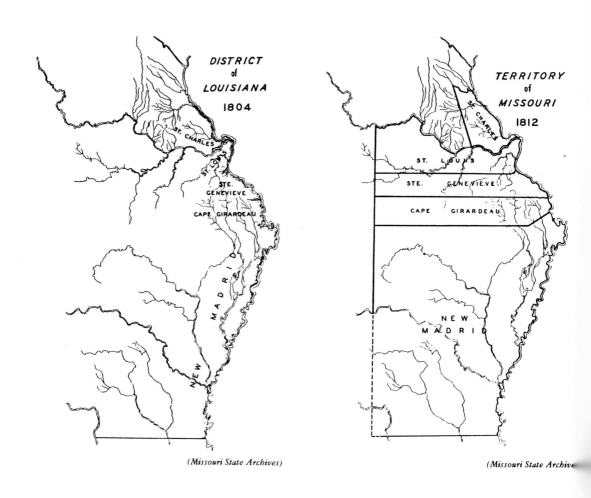

(Missouri State Archives)   *(Missouri State Archive*

Counties evolved as the Territory of Missouri moved toward statehood.

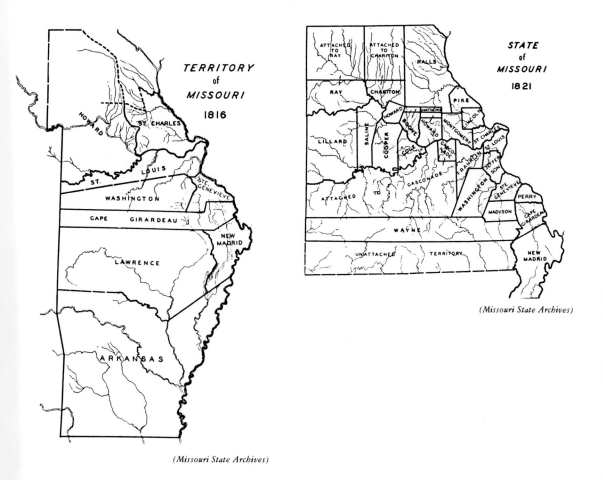

(Missouri State Archives)

(Missouri State Archives)

In 1820, John Hardiman Walker, a prominent landowner near present-day Caruthersville, was influential in the "bootheel's" addition to the southeastern boundary of Missouri.

In 1836, by the annexation of the Platte Purchase, Missouri extended its northwest boundaries (not shown). All land west of the 1821 boundary to the Missouri River was added as a result of a treaty with the Indian tribes living in the area (the Iowas, and the Missouri band of the Sacs and Foxes).

Missouri Enabling Act

On March 16, 1818, and again on December 18, 1818, the territorial legislature made application to Congress for the passage of a law that would authorize the people of the Territory of Missouri to organize a state government.

But the Missouri statehood matter became embroiled in controversy. On February 13, 1819, the bill came before the House of Representatives that would enable the people of Missouri to form a state government prior to admission into the Union. James Tallmadge of New York presented an amendment to this bill that prohibited further introduction of slaves into Missouri, and provided that all children of slave parents born in the state after its admission should be free at age 25. The House passed the bill on February 17, but the Senate did not agree, and the measure was lost with the adjournment of the Fifteenth Congress.

When Congress reconvened in December 1819, the petition was again introduced in the House. Up to 1818, in order to maintain a balance of power in Congress, new states had been admitted in pairs, a free state with a slave state. Maine, then a part of Massachusetts, was seeking statehood as a free state. The Maine bill was passed by the House and sent to the Senate on January 3, 1820. The Missouri bill without slave restrictions was added to the Maine bill as an amendment. This Maine-Missouri bill was taken up by the Senate on January 13.[10]

Senator Jonathan Roberts of Pennsylvania immediately introduced an amendment which stated that the State of Missouri would not be admitted to the Union unless its constitution prohibited slavery.[11] This failed to pass. On February 3, Sen. J. B. Thomas of Illinois offered a second amendment that excluded slavery from the Louisiana Purchase north of 36 degrees and 30 minutes north latitude (the southern boundary of Missouri), except within the limits of the proposed State of Missouri. On February 17, the Maine-Missouri bill with the Thomas amendment passed the Senate.

The House refused to accept the bill. They separated the Maine and Missouri portions, and passed the Maine bill. Henry Clay of Kentucky, a popular and influential Speaker of the House of Representatives, persuaded the majority of members to accept the Missouri bill with the Thomas amendment.

On March 2, 1820, the Missouri Enabling Act was passed. It included the Thomas amendment which excluded slavery above the 36^0 30', except for Missouri. It provided that the people of Missouri could draw up a constitution, form a state government, and choose a name. The people of Missouri were granted one United States Representative based on the census of 1820. It set the boundaries of the state, provided for the election of representatives to a constitutional convention, and set the date for the constitutional convention for the second Monday in June. The Enabling Act offered several proposals for the use of land based on the state's agreement to certain tax restrictions on the sale of public lands. In addition, it required that a certified copy of the state constitution be submitted to Congress.[12]

On March 3, 1820, President Monroe signed the bill admitting Maine as a free state; and on March 6, signed the Missouri Enabling Act, admitting Missouri with no slavery restrictions.[13] The passage of these bills became known as the Missouri Compromise.

Constitutional Convention

The forty-one delegates to the first state constitutional convention were elected on the first Monday and two succeeding days of May 1820.

The convention met on June 12 in St. Louis in the Mansion House Hotel located at Third and Vine Streets.[14] St. Louis was the largest town in the state. (A census taken by John W. Thompson in 1815 showed a total population of 7,395 for the county and town, and 2,000 inhabitants of the town itself.)

The delegates gave the state the by-then-familiar name Missouri, an Indian word meaning "he of the big canoe."[15]

The convention concluded on July 19, 1820, with the signing of the Missouri constitution.

The constitution provided for 14 senators and 43 representatives, and required the first General Assembly to meet on the third Monday in September 1820 in St. Louis. This meeting of Missouri's first government was held at the Missouri Hotel, located at Main and Morgan Streets.[16]

Statehood

When Missouri's constitution was presented to Congress in 1821, heated debates ensued concerning the constitutionality of the twenty-sixth section of the third article. It required the legislature to pass a law, or laws, to prevent Negroes and mulattoes from coming into, or settling in the state, on any pretext.

On February 26, 1821, a joint committee of the House and Senate reached an agreement that Missouri was to be admitted under her constitution when she pledged, by a solemn public act, never to construe that clause so as to authorize any law that would deprive the rights of citizens of any other state. The solemn public act demanded by Congress was passed, and on August 10, 1821, President Monroe issued a proclamation completing the admission of Missouri into the Union. It was the first state formed from the northern part of the Louisiana Purchase.

Missouri permitted slavery until January 11, 1865. The Emancipation Proclamation of Missouri was passed three weeks before the Thirteenth Amendment to the United States Constitution was proposed by Congress.[17]

Part III

Missouri's Capitols

Capitols Move West

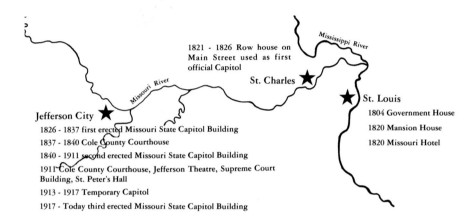

1821 - 1826 Row house on Main Street used as first official Capitol

St. Charles

Mississippi River

Missouri River

St. Louis

1804 Government House

1820 Mansion House

1820 Missouri Hotel

Jefferson City

1826 - 1837 first erected Missouri State Capitol Building
1837 - 1840 Cole County Courthouse
1840 - 1911 second erected Missouri State Capitol Building
1911 Cole County Courthouse, Jefferson Theatre, Supreme Court Building, St. Peter's Hall
1913 - 1917 Temporary Capitol
1917 - Today third erected Missouri State Capitol Building

The State of Missouri has conducted official business from a total of 13 buildings, from the first territorial Government House, built in St. Louis in 1768, to today's marble masterpiece.

During early statehood, some of the Capitols were rented for only a short session or two. Later, as the state grew, so did the need for new Capitols, and in each case, Missourians built a Capitol to suit the needs of the period.

Reasons for building new Capitols in Missouri range from relocation of the capital city, through obsolescence, to raging fire.

The brief pictorial review on these pages is a serial glimpse of the history of those state houses which have served the Show-Me State.

St. Louis - 1820

(Missouri State Archives)

(Missouri State Archives)

Top: The Mansion House served as Missouri's headquarters for the first constitutional convention in June 1820.

Bottom: Missouri's first General Assembly met in the Missouri Hotel in September 1820.

(Missouri State Archives)

A row house in St. Charles served as Missouri's first official state Capitol from 1821-1826. It has been restored as a state historic site by the Missouri Department of Natural Resources.

St. Charles - 1821

The Temporary Capital City

In 1820, St. Charles was a town of approximately 1,200 residents, near the center of population and located near the junction of the Missouri and Mississippi rivers. Many towns were proposed for the site of the temporary capital city. The fact that St. Charles offered to provide the General Assembly and its committees accommodations free of charge might have been the deciding factor in its selection.[1] On November 25, 1820, Governor McNair signed a bill which fixed a temporary seat of government at St. Charles.[2]

In June 1821, the legislature moved to a temporary Capitol on Main Street in St. Charles. On Monday, November 6, 1821, the first session of the General Assembly met. For the next five years the entire second story of the row house served as the state headquarters.

Establishing the Permanent Capital City

The bill signed by Governor McNair on November 25, 1820, also provided for five commissioners, one from each corner of the state and one from the center, to locate a site for Missouri's capital city. They were guided by article ten of the 1820 constitution, which stipulated that the capital of Missouri should be located on the banks of the Missouri River within forty miles of the mouth of the Osage River. The reasons for these restrictions were simple. With the only centers of population located on the Missouri and Mississippi rivers, the major means of transportation was by riverboat. Also, a central location for the capital would provide the easiest access to those living in the inland area.

The location at the confluence of the Osage and the Missouri Rivers, Cote Sans Dessein, was also considered, but confusion over land titles resulted in a vote against that location. On December 31, 1821, the General Assembly chose a site for Missouri's capital,[3] and on January 11, 1822, named the capital city the "City of Jefferson."

The city's location is described in "Reminiscences, June 24, 1826" of the December 6, 1871, *Jefferson City Peoples Tribune:*

> It is located in Cole County, on the south shore of the Missouri, twelve hundred miles from New Orleans, one hundred and twenty-five from St. Louis, one hundred and twenty from the junction of the Mississippi and the Missouri, and ten above the mouth of the Osage.

The commissioners applied for and obtained a governmental land grant in the region of Lohman's Landing for the specific purpose of establishing a seat of government. Lohman's Landing was built in 1834, and is one of the oldest standing buildings in Missouri. The area abounded with river and wagon traffic, and was a ferry station for traffic across the Missouri River. The *Jefferson City Peoples Tribune* article also described the lots:

> There were 1,000 small lots containing half an acre each, over an area of about half of a square mile. The number of large lots lying more remote is not known. In May 1823, two hundred of the small lots were sold at public auction.

Two families lived in Jefferson City at that time, those of Josiah Ramsey and William Jones.

The move of the capital from St. Charles to Jefferson City was set for October 1, 1826, just five years after Missouri was admitted to the Union.

The first Capitol in Jefferson City housed the legislature and served as the governor's residence. Previous to 1955, no drawing was known to exist. In that year, Marcel Boulicault, a St. Louis architect, sketched his conception of the 1826 structure.

Jefferson City - 1826

The First Capitol - 1826

Jefferson City's first Capitol was the first building erected for the express purpose of being the State Capitol of Missouri. It was constructed on the site now occupied by the Executive Mansion, and was completed in two years at a cost of $18,573. The legislature appropriated the funds on February 8, 1825, to pay James Dunnica and Daniel Colgan for the building's construction. This Capitol housed not only the House of Representatives and the Senate, but was also the governor's residence until 1834 when the first Executive Mansion was completed.

This two-story state house was described in the November 18, 1826, *Jeffersonian Republican,* "The Governor's House":

> This house was only intended to be occupied by the legislature till a state house could be erected. It is a spacious and well constructed building; the workmanship, it is said, is not surpassed in the state. It stands fronting the Missouri, on an eminence of 200 feet above the level of the waters. Its dimensions are 60 feet by 40 . . . There are ten commodious rooms . . . a stairway runs from the bottom to the top and opens through a skylight into the ballastrade or large platform surrounded by a railing . . .

This Capitol burned in 1837. The *Jeffersonian Republican,* Saturday, November 18, 1837, described the events:

> On Wednesday evening last, about nine o'clock, flames were seen bursting from the window of the north room of the State House, on the second floor, occupied by the Secretary of State. Every exertion was made by our citizens to extinguish the flames, but to no effect, there being no fire engines in the city. In a very short time the whole office was wrapt in flames, and no hope was left for arresting the progress. The books and papers of the Auditor's office and a part of the State Library, was with difficulty saved. Nothing was saved from the office of the Secretary of State . . . including the state seal . . . not even the smallest article of furniture. The destruction of the records of this office may be considered a great public loss.

The November 25, 1837, *Jeffersonian Republican,* pleaded for the formation of a fire company:

> It would certainly be well for our citizens to form a fire company under discipline sufficient to form a line to the river, in case of accident by fire. As might be expected in a place visited for the first time by this terrific element, the greatest confusion prevailed at the recent fire. Scores of men were seen running towards the scene without buckets . . . The forming of such a company would consume little time, and be attended with no expense to its members, except the furnishing by each of a fire bucket.

Jefferson City's Cole County Courthouse served as the temporary Capitol for three years.

(Suden's Souvenir of Jefferson City, MO. owned by Dr. J. S. Summers, Jr.)

The Cole County Courthouse served as a temporary Capitol from 1837-1840.

(Cole County Historical Socie...

The 1840 Capitol faced the southeast, high on a hill above the Missouri River. It towered majestically over the struggling, but growing town.

The Second Capitol - 1840

Plans for a new Capitol were approved by the ninth General Assembly on February 2, 1837, nine months before the fire that destroyed the first Capitol building. The location for the new structure was designated as "Capitol Hill," the first hill west of the first Capitol.[4]

An appropriation of $75,000 was given for the construction of the second Capitol. The architect was A. Stephen Hills. It was adequate for the General Assembly and the executive departments, "and, shall be, as far as practicable, fireproof, inside and outside, especially the offices of the state; the building shall be covered with sheet copper or lead, and executed interiorly of brick, and exteriorly of stone."[5]

This Capitol was built facing Jefferson Street. The interior was brick, the exterior stone. It accommodated the House of Representatives, the Senate, a state library, executive rooms and state offices.

The *Jeffersonian Republican,* May 5, 1838, described the building in the article, "The New State House":

> The ground work of this building being completed, we have had the pleasure during the past week of seeing the commencement of the outer walls, which are to be hammered rock to the basement, and then they are to be polished. As far as this work has progressed, it has an elegant, durable appearance. The contractor, Mr. Withnell, instead of quarrying rock from the river, obtains them three fourths of a mile back of town from an out lot where they are said to be of a very superior quality, and of a white color, and much better adapted to the kind of work for which they are wanted.

The situation of this building in size 158 by 81 [feet], 2 stories high, and on a high bluff, commanding a view of the river for 8 miles up and down, must when completed, give it a very beautiful appearance; for not even the first tier of stone above the ground work can be hid from the river. It is arranged to front south [southeast, facing Jefferson Street], with a noble circular portico of three columns, towering the whole length of the building, with a dome above the roof.

The limestone for the pillars was from Callaway County.

In 1838 Governor Boggs calmly informed the Assembly that $125,000 beyond the original appropriation would be needed to complete the building. In fact, the total expenditures incurred brought the total to almost $292,000, which included $30,000 for the grounds.[6]

(Postcard owned by Dr. J. S. Summers, f

The 1840 Capitol was remodeled in 1887-1888. The dome was raised and wings were added.

Capitol Remodeled 1887-1888

After the Civil War, additions to the structure were necessary. On January 10, 1877, the *Jefferson City Peoples Tribune* ran an article, "Plans for Improving the Capitol."

> Mr. Harry Kemp, architect of this city, has prepared a plan for the improvement of the Capitol, so as to give larger and better halls for the Senate and House of Representatives, and Supreme Court rooms and offices.
>
> The plan proceeds upon the idea that the terrace on which the Capitol stands is to be graded until the basement story will be above ground, and be made dry, and of some use. Wings, 76 by 114 feet, are to be added to the north and south end[s] of the present building . . . The present dome which is going to decay is to be replaced by one of iron, to be made to correspond to the enlarged condition of the building.
>
> The estimated cost of the whole is to be $140,000.

In 1887 an act was passed and approved by the governor appropriating $259,000 to enlarge and render fireproof the state Capitol, build fireproof vaults and provide a heating system, all to be completed by January 1, 1889.[7]

In 1887-1888, two wings were built in a T-shape on the north and south. Each wing was 109 feet by 76 feet, so the Capitol was enlarged to 300 feet long and 112 feet wide. A new dome 185 feet high towered over the structure.[8] The remodeling of this Capitol cost the state $263,218.28[9] (almost as much as the original structure, and more than $123,000 over architect Harry Kemp's estimate).

The Senate Chamber occupied some of the old rooms which were enlarged and redecorated.

The Jefferson City Daily Tribune of June 20, 1889, reported that the communications were very inadequate in the Capitol. There was one telephone in the entire building, in the governor's office.

> The great and wealthy state of Missouri certainly can afford to pay telephone tolls for each department, and it would seem a little more modern and in accordance with the fitness of things if they were promptly supplied with the instruments.

The heat for this remodeled building was supplied by a central heating plant built in 1905 for $35,000. This plant was located directly north of the Capitol below the river bluff, and benefited from direct access to the railroad. Three large boilers, 100 horsepower each, generated the heat that was conveyed by tunnels to the Capitol building, the Armory, the new Supreme Court building and the Governor's Mansion.

Electric power for the lighting was generated at the penitentiary.[10]

As early as 1901, arguments for a new Capitol were surfacing. The *Jefferson City Daily Press,* April 19, 1901, presented their feelings:

> Missouri needs a new Capitol building. The present old structure, built in 1838 and added to in 1887, is wholly inadequate for the purposes of the state . . . besides being old, unsightly and thirty

years behind most of the states of this Union. It will probably take
ten years to get . . . Missouri should have a Capitol building built of
Missouri material, costing not less than $3,000,000 and the
Legislature of 1911, or the Forty-sixth General Assembly, must
meet within its walls!

In 1910 a major campaign was waged for a modern state house. This
new building would have been provided by the proposed fifth
constitutional amendment that was rejected by popular vote.[11]

On February 5, 1911, this second Capitol burned.

A year of indecision followed. Should the ruins be repaired or a
temporary Capitol be built? Because of legal action brought in May 1912
by W. C. Irwin, chief clerk in the secretary of state's office, the legislature
was forced to build a temporary Capitol.[12]

The temporary Capitol was built in 1912 at a cost of $77,427. It was torn down in 1917 when the present Capitol was completed.

The Temporary Capitol - 1913

In June 1912, a temporary Capitol was recommended by the Capitol Commission. Total cost of the structure, including furnishings, was $77,427. Government officials and the 47th General Assembly moved into the temporary Capitol in January 1913.[13] Erected in three months, it was situated directly south of the second Capitol on Stewart Street, and was mostly wooden. The 1916 Sanborn Map shows this as a stucco structure, which was smoothed to resemble stone.

An article on December 29, 1915, in the *Daily Capitol News* headlined:

STATE OFFICIALS ARE THREATENED WITH DROWNING

Leaky Roof on Temporary Capitol
Flooding Every Office in Building

Wanted, Immediately - All of the tin tubs, buckets, cuspidors, dishpans and rain barrels that I can get to catch the water that drips through the roof of the temporary Capitol. Bring them at once before the governor and all of the state officials are drowned.

John Scott,
Commissioner Permanent Seat of Government

John Scott, Commissioner of the Permanent Seat of Government, is battling valliantly with water which is dripping through the roof of the temporary Capitol and flooding the House and Senate Chambers.

From here it percolates gently through the ceilings and precipitates itself unfeelingly upon the heads of the governor or other officials while they are engrossed perchance in the problems of state.

Since the snow fell, Scott and his force have been busy rustling pans, spittoons, tubs, buckets, etc. to catch the water as it drips through the roof.

When not hunting new receptacles for water, Scott and his force were busy emptying the full ones. When the hour for dinner arrived yesterday one man was sent for sandwiches while others bailed.

It is estimated there are about 30 tons more of snow upon the roof which reduced to water, equals a very large number of gallons.

Scott and his helpers were unable to shovel the snow off because of the ice and the rottenness of the roofing. They feared if they attempted to get the snow off, the roof would come with it.

This building served as the temporary Capitol until October 1917 when it was torn down.[14]

Capitols Location Map

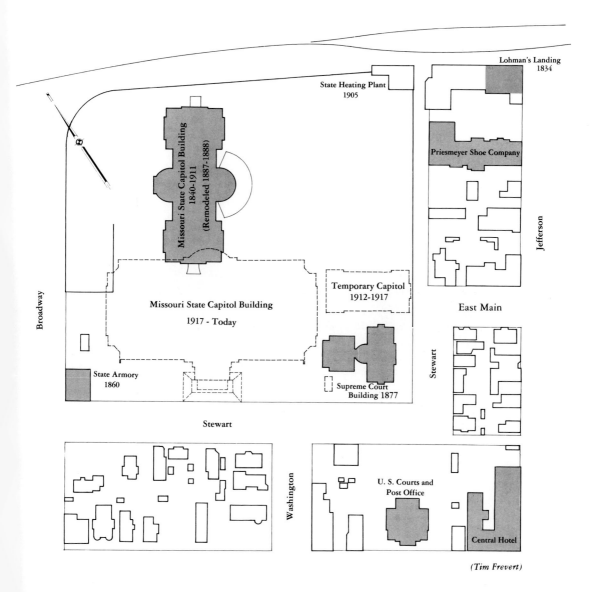

State Heating Plant
1905

Lohman's Landing
1834

Priesmeyer Shoe Company

Jefferson

Missouri State Capitol Building
1840-1911
(Remodeled 1887-1888)

Temporary Capitol
1912-1917

East Main

Broadway

Missouri State Capitol Building

1917 - Today

Stewart

State Armory
1860

Supreme Court
Building 1877

Stewart

Washington

U. S. Courts and
Post Office

Central Hotel

(Tim Frevert)

The Sanborn Insurance Maps of 1908 and 1916 owned by Dr. J. S. Summers, Jr.
provided the locations of the 1840 Capitol, the temporary Capitol and the present
Capitol.

In 1917 the State Armory (left) was still in use. Buildings along Stewart Street had been demolished to make room for the expanded Capitol grounds.

The Third Capitol - 1917

This state house, present today, is the second Capitol to parallel the Missouri River. The first Capitol of 1826 also faced the river.

Bills were introduced in the Senate and the House of Representatives on February 7, 1911,[15] to provide for a bond issue of $3.5 million to build this new Capitol; $3.0 million for use in erecting a new State Capitol, $300,000 for furnishings and $200,000 to purchase additional ground.[16] The floor space of the burned out Capitol had been approximately 50,000 square feet. The proposed new building provided for 300,000 square feet plus nearly three acres in the sub-basement. At a special election on August 1, 1911, the people ratified the measure by a vote of 144,664 to 45,468.[17]

On October 6, 1911, the State Capitol Commission was organized.

A preliminary contest for choice of an architect was held with 69 architects competing. The ten best were chosen by a board and an advisory jury. On October 6, 1912, Evarts Tracy and Egerton Swartwout of New York were chosen.[18]

In the February 1927 issue of *The Architectural Record,* Mr. Swartwout stated:

> The old Capitol for some reason stood end on to the river, perhaps to give a better view to the Pen, and there were on the site several old brick buildings which probably served some purpose or other, and there was, when I saw it first, a temporary Capitol of wood and stucco, and between and around these buildings were a great number of magnificent elms, there being quite a grove of them

down in one corner by the river. And the sad thing about it was we had to cut them all down. We couldn't demolish the old buildings until the new Capitol was built, and as it was determined to put the new building parallel to the river, the trees had to go. It was a great pity, and that's the reason the surroundings look so bare at the present time [1927]. I always thought, and I think most of the Commission thought, it would have been much better to have sold the old site and built on one of the hills outside the town.[19]

The rules of the architect's competition program dictated the basic plan for the Capitol. Swartwout continued:

> The legislative chambers face each other on each side of the central rotunda, and are on what is really the third floor; the offices for state officials are on the two lower floors.[20]

> The dome is of stone and is, as I remember, about 300 feet high, and if anyone is courageous and strong enough to climb up, there is a very wonderful view from the top of it. I went up once or twice but it was a complicated climb after leaving the elevator and there is a story that my partner, Col. Evarts Tracy, once tried to take a party of visitors up there before the building was finished, and got completely lost between the roofs.[21]

On May 6, 1913, work on the foundation was started; it was completed in December.[22]

On August 12, 1914, the steelworkers held a flag raising ceremony on top of the steel structure, signifying completion of the steelwork. The 25 officials and steelworkers who participated in the ceremony were hoisted to the top of the structure on a boat-like platform.

(Missouri State Archives)

Over five thousand tons of steel were used in the framework of the Capitol. Steelwork was completed by August 1914.

Skilled workmen from New York prepared molds and forms for the concrete used in the superstructure of the building.

The cornerstone ceremony for the new building was held June 24, 1915.[23]

(Dr. J. S. Summers, Jr.)

The Senate and House of the Forty-ninth Assembly held formal meetings in their respective chambers on March 16, 1917.[24]

On September 8, 1917, four years and four months after the groundbreaking ceremony, the Capitol was ready for occupancy. However, it was not until much of the exterior and interior artwork was complete, that the Capitol was dedicated.

The dedication celebration, held October 6, 1924, was an all-day affair. It started with a parade at 11:00 a.m. followed by a band concert at 1:00 p.m. The dedication ceremony started at 2:00 p.m. with a welcome by the mayor, and was followed by addresses from five ex-governors, an address by the current Governor Arthur M. Hyde, and the reading of a message from President Calvin Coolidge. A release of carrier pigeons announced to the world that Missouri's new Capitol had been dedicated.[25]

(Joseph R. Kroeger, Sr.)

Cole County was one of 114 counties that entered a float in the dedication day parade.

The State National Guard marched in the parade, and the Army dirigible TC-5 flew overhead.

(Joseph R. Kroeger, Sr.)

Daily Capital News, October 8, 1924: "A vast crowd of Missourians came here yesterday from all sections of the state. The great audience spread over more than 10,000 seats placed upon the front lawn of the state house, overflowed upon the terraces, stood in the driveways, the main street of the city at the south edge of the Capitol grounds, and swarmed over the steps and lawn of the Missouri Supreme Court Building, which faces the Capitol from across the street."

(Joseph R. Kroeger, S

(Ron Arsenault)

An aerial photo taken from a biplane on Capitol Dedication Day, October 6, 1924, shows a flourishing capital city.

The year 1988 will mark the 71st anniversary of the functional use of our present Capitol. During that year, this Capitol will match the length of service of the Capitol which burned in 1911.

With the knowledge we gained from the 1911 Capitol fire, with technological advances, and with a statewide dedication to preserve the past for the future, let us work to keep this proud monument to Missouri for decades to come.

Joseph S. Summers, Jr.

Notes

Part II - Missouri and Statehood

1. David D. March, *The History of Missouri,* 151.
2. Ibid., 160.
3. Floyd C. Shoemaker, *Missouri and Missourians,* 168.
4. March, *The History of Missouri,* 159.
5. Ibid.
6. Duane G. Meyer, *The Heritage of Missouri,* 117.
7. March, *The History of Missouri,* 165.
8. *Encyclopedia Britannica,* 14th ed., s.v. "Arkansas."
9. Ibid., s.v. "Iowa" and "Minnesota."
10. March, *The History of Missouri,* 393.
11. Ibid.
12. Shoemaker, *Missouri and Missourians,* 177, 178.
13. *Encyclopedia Britannica,* s.v. "Missouri Compromise."
14. Marian M. Ohman, *The History of Missouri Capitols,* 6.
15. Shoemaker, *Missouri and Missourians,* 3.
16. Ohman, *The History of Missouri Capitols,* 9.
17. March, *The History of Missouri,* 999.

Part III - Missouri's Capitols

1. Jonas Viles, "The Capitals and Capitols of Missouri," *Missouri Historical Review,* 1918-1919, vol. 13, 1st article, sec. 4, 144.
2. David D. March, *The History of Missouri,* 441.
3. Viles, *Missouri Historical Review,* sec. 6, 150.
4. "Capitol Burns in 1911," *Capital City Telephone Directory,* 1968.
5. Viles, *Missouri Historical Review,* 1918-1919, vol. 13, 2nd article, sec. 8, 238.
6. Ibid., 239, 241.
7. Ibid., 242.
8. "Capitol Burns," *Capital City Telephone Directory.*

9. Viles, *Missouri Historical Review,* 243.
10. "Capitol Burns," *Capital City Telephone Directory.*
11. Ibid.
12. Marian M. Ohman, *The History of Missouri Capitols,* 57.
13. Ibid., 59.
14. Ibid.
15. "Capitol Burns," *Capital City Telephone Directory.*
16. Viles, *Missouri Historical Review,* sec. 9, 247.
17. "Capitol Burns," *Capital City Telephone Directory.*
18. Viles, *Missouri Historical Review,* 248.
19. Egerton Swartwout, "The Missouri State Capitol," *The Architectural Record,* February 1927, Vol. 61, 108.
20. Ibid., 119.
21. Ibid., 120.
22. Viles, *Missouri Historical Review,* 248.
23. "Capitol Burns," *Capital City Telephone Directory.*
24. Viles, *Missouri Historical Review,* 249.
25. "Capitol Burns," *Capital City Telephone Directory.*

Select Bibliography

Articles

"An Unique and Informative Feature." *State of Missouri Official Manual* (1943-1944) : 1130-1136.

"Capitol Burns in 1911." *Capital City Telephone Directory* (1968).

"Fire Departments." *The Illustrated Sketch Book, 1900* : 33.

House and Senate Journals of the 47th General Assembly State of Missouri, vol. 1 (1913) : 17-19.

Selinger, Msgr. Joseph. *Missouri Valley Fire Chief's Journal* (April-May 1951) : 28.

Swartwout, Egerton. "The Missouri State Capitol." *The Architectural Record* (1927) : 105-120.

Viles, Jonas. "Lessons to be Learned from the Fire of the State Capitol, Jefferson City." *American Historical Review* (1911) : 337-342.

Viles, Jonas. "Missouri Capitals and Capitols." *Missouri Historical Review* (1918-1919) : 135-155, 232-250.

Books

Davis, Walter B., and Daniel S. Durrie. *An Illustrated History of Missouri.* St. Louis: A. J. Hall and Company, 1876.

March, David D. *The History of Missouri.* New York: Lewis Historical Publishing Company, 1967.

The Encyclopedia Britannica. 14th ed., New York: Encyclopedia Britannica, Inc., 1938.

Meyer, Duane G. *The Heritage of Missouri.* 2 vol. St. Louis: River City Publishers, Ltd., 1982.

Ohman, Marian M. *The History of Missouri Capitols.* Columbia: University of Missouri, 1982.

Park, Eleanora G., and Kate S. Morrow. *Women of the Mansion, Missouri, 1821-1936.* Jefferson City: Midland Printing Company, 1936.

Shoemaker, Floyd C. *Missouri and Missourians.* 2 vol. Chicago: Lewis Publishing Company, 1943.

Williams, Walter. *The State of Missouri.* Columbia: Press of E. W. Stephens, 1904.

Newspapers

Jefferson City:

> *Jeffersonian Republican* (November 18, 1826; November 18, 1827; November 25, 1827; May 5, 1838)
>
> *Peoples Tribune* (December 6, 1871; January 10, 1877)
>
> *Daily Tribune* (June 20, 1889)
>
> *Daily Press* (April 19, 1901; December 29, 1915)
>
> *Capital News* (February 6, 1911)
>
> *Democrat-Tribune* (date unknown)
>
> *Post* (February 7, 1911)
>
> *Post Tribune* (February 5, 1952)

Sedalia:

> *Democrat-Sentinel* (February 6, 1911)
>
> *Daily Capital* (date unknown)

Kansas City Post (February 6, 1911)

Kirksville Democrat (February 10, 1911)

St. Louis Post Dispatch (February 6, 1911)

Springfield Leader (February 6, 1911)